Amusement Parks Around America

Lorin Driggs

Consultant

Brian Allman
Principal
Upshur County Schools, West Virginia

Publishing Credits

Rachelle Cracchiolo, M.S.Ed., *Publisher*
Emily R. Smith, M.A.Ed., *SVP of Content Development*
Véronique Bos, *VP of Creative*
Dona Herweck Rice, *Senior Content Manager*
Dani Neiley, *Editor*
Fabiola Sepulveda, *Series Graphic Designer*

Image Credits: p6 Alamy Stock Photo/Incamerastock; p8 Getty Images/Science & Society Picture Library; p9 (top) Alamy Stock Photo/Heritage Image Partnership Ltd; p9 (bottom) Library of Congress [LC-USZ62-50927]; p10 Boston Public Library Tichnor Brothers collection #65588; p13 (top) Alamy Stock Photo/Paul Briden; p13 (bottom) Shutterstock/Juan Camilo Bernal; p14 Alamy Stock Photo/Pictorial Press Ltd; p15 Alamy Stock Photo/Everett Collection Incl; p16 Getty Images/Pictorial Parade; p17 (top) Courtesy Fabiola Sepulveda; p17 (bottom) Alamy Stock Photo/Greg Balfour Evans; pp18-19 Shutterstock/Jerome Labouyrie; p19 (bottom) Shutterstock/Chuck Wagner; p22 (top) Shutterstock/Craig Russell; p22 (bottom) Shutterstock/Sarunyu L; p23 Alamy Stock Photo/Stephen Saks Photography; p24 Alamy Stock Photo/Yvette Cardozo; p25 Alamy Stock Photo/stephen Searle; p25 (left) National Archives/Department of the Interior. Patent Office. (1849 - 1925); p25 (right) National Archives/Department of the Interior. Patent Office. (1849 - 1925); p27 Shutterstock/Studio Melange; p32 Shutterstock/Sherry V Smith; all other images from iStock and/or Shutterstock

Library of Congress Cataloging-in-Publication Data

Names: Driggs, Lorin, author.
Title: Amusement parks around America / Lorin Driggs.
Description: Huntington Beach, CA : Teacher Created Materials, 2023. | Includes index. | Audience: Grades 4-6 | Summary: "People have enjoyed amusement parks in the United States for almost 200 years. Where did they begin? How have they changed? The answers are interesting! Learn how the first theme park started with berries. And discover how Walt Disney changed the idea of amusement parks for the world"-- Provided by publisher.
Identifiers: LCCN 2022021315 (print) | LCCN 2022021316 (ebook) | ISBN 9781087691138 (paperback) | ISBN 9781087691299 (ebook)
Subjects: LCSH: Amusement parks--United States--History--Juvenile literature.
Classification: LCC GV1853.2 .D75 2023 (print) | LCC GV1853.2 (ebook) | DDC 791.06/873--dc23/eng/20220601
LC record available at https://lccn.loc.gov/2022021315
LC ebook record available at https://lccn.loc.gov/2022021316

Shown on the cover is the Mako roller coaster in Orlando, Florida.

This book may not be reproduced or distributed in any way without prior written consent from the publisher.

TCM | Teacher Created Materials

5482 Argosy Avenue
Huntington Beach, CA 92649
www.tcmpub.com

ISBN 978-1-0876-9113-8

© 2023 Teacher Created Materials, Inc.

Table of Contents

Some Words about Words

What exactly is an amusement park? It helps to know what *amuse* means. The definition is "to entertain" or "to make someone laugh or smile." So then, that is what amusement parks are supposed to do.

The United States has plenty of these amusing places. Before taking a closer look at amusement parks around the United States, let's answer a couple of questions.

What is the difference between amusement parks and theme parks? Actually, theme parks *are* amusement parks. Like all amusement parks, theme parks have rides and other fun features, such as roller coasters, merry-go-rounds, and places to get food. The difference is that all the rides and features in theme parks have something in common. The thing in common is their theme. The theme might have something to do with movies, holidays, the ocean, a particular place, or even a company or a product.

Navy Pier, an amusement park in Chicago

A Fair Deal

There are an estimated 2,000 county and state fairs in the United States. They are an American tradition dating to the early 1800s. Originally, they focused on **agriculture**. Farmers could buy and sell livestock and farm products. Over time, entertainment features and competitions were added.

Are fairs and carnivals also amusement parks? No! This answer is much easier. Amusement parks stay in one place and are there all the time. Fairs and carnivals come and go. Carnivals, especially, travel from place to place. They stay for a short time and then move on.

carnival in West Windsor, New Jersey

Bit of "Amusing" History

The idea of amusement parks has been around for a long time. It first started more than 1,000 years ago.

Fairs

Communities in Asia and Europe had what we now call fairs. They usually happened on special days, often religious holidays. The purpose then was not to have fun. It was to buy and sell things. But sellers realized that if people had a good time, they might stay longer. And if they stayed longer, they might buy more. So, sellers had the idea of hiring entertainers to perform. There were jugglers, acrobats, magicians, and singers.

Pleasure Gardens

In the 1700s, "pleasure gardens" were England's idea of amusement parks. English cities at that time were crowded, noisy, and dirty. To get away, people would pay a small **fee** to enter a beautiful garden. They could **stroll** among the flowers and have picnics. They could even enjoy fireworks, a concert, or some other kind of entertainment. Vauxhall was the first of these gardens.

Vauxhall Gardens

World's Fairs

Then came world's fairs. They displayed new products and new ways of having fun. The earliest such fair was held in 1851 in London, England. The World's Columbian **Exposition** of 1893 was the first world's fair in the United States. It took place in Chicago, Illinois. It is also known as the Chicago World's Fair. It featured products, food, and entertainment from around the world.

If You Dare...

The World's Columbian Exposition of 1893 offered plenty of thrills. A fairgoer could ride an ostrich or a camel, float up in a hot-air balloon, or zoom along an ice-covered track on the Ice Railway.

Chicago World's Fair

Rides are a big part of amusement park fun. The following three are among the oldest rides. They are still very popular.

Merry-Go-Round or Carousel

These rides are usually beautiful and gentle. But *carousel* comes from a word that means "little war." Long ago, warriors in Europe and Asia practiced their skills by riding their horses in a circle. That is why early merry-go-rounds featured horses. Today, you might ride an elephant, a pig, a rabbit, a chicken, or even an alligator.

merry-go-round, about 1910, England

Flying Mountain roller coaster, 1815, Ukraine

Roller Coaster

Some say the idea for modern roller coasters came from Russia. In the 17th century, Russians built high steep **slopes** out of wood. In winter, they sprayed the slopes with water. The water froze on the surface. People climbed stairs to the top. They got into sleds. Down they went, sliding on the ice all the way to the bottom. These old ice slides were fun. They were even scary. But modern roller coasters are huge and elaborate. And they are often very scary!

Ferris Wheel

George Ferris invented the Ferris wheel. He built it for the World's Columbian Exposition of 1893. The first one had 36 cars that could carry as many as 60 people. These giant spinning wheels are still among the most popular amusement park rides.

Ferris wheel, 1893, Chicago

Oldies but Goodies

Amusement parks have been part of American life for almost 200 years. Some of the oldest ones are still around. They continue to bring laughter and thrills.

Lake Compounce, Bristol, Connecticut

Lake Compounce holds the record. It is America's oldest amusement park. It opened as a picnic park in 1846. Over time, rides were added. A carousel arrived in 1911. It had horses, of course. It also had one goat. A roller coaster called the Wildcat was built in 1927. You can still ride that carousel and that roller coaster.

Lake Compounce, Bristol, Connecticut

Cedar Point, Sandusky, Ohio

This park opened in 1870. The only way to get there was by ferry. That was true for more than 80 years. Its first roller coaster, the Switchback Railway, opened in 1892. By 2021, it had 17 roller coasters! It is known as the Roller Coaster Capital of the World.

Coney Island, Brooklyn, New York

Coney Island is famous for many reasons. It had the first roller coaster in America, opening in 1884. Its top speed was six miles (about 10 kilometers) per hour. Coney Island is also famous for the hot dog. This American food was invented there. Coney Island is special in other ways, too. It has an annual mermaid parade. And of course, it has an annual hot-dog-eating contest.

Coney Island, Brooklyn, New York

Who Invented the Hot Dog?

Charles Feltman had a sausage stand on Coney Island in 1867. People loved the sausages, but eating them required a plate and silverware. His solution was to wrap them in a sliced roll so people could enjoy them while strolling along the boardwalk.

Dorney Park, Allentown, Pennsylvania

In 1870, Solomon Dorney turned his property into a public park. The park had playground rides, games, and a small zoo. A ride called the Whip was added in 1920. It is still in operation. Dorney Park now has seven roller coasters, including its first, Thunderhawk, which has been operating since 1923.

Knott's Berry Farm, Buena Park, California

First, there was a farm growing berries. Then, there was a market selling the berries. Then, there was a tea room serving jams and pies made with the berries. Then, there was a restaurant that became famous for its fried chicken. The fried chicken was so popular that people had to wait hours to get into the restaurant. To entertain them, the Knott family built a replica of an old western ghost town. People started coming just to see the Ghost Town. The family expanded the Ghost Town over the years. More buildings, a museum, a copy of the Liberty Bell, and a log **flume** ride were added. Knott's Berry Farm had become America's first theme park. Its theme was the Old West, and that theme remains a large section of the park.

A New Berry

The boysenberry was created by Rudolph Boysen. It is a cross between a raspberry, a blackberry, and a dewberry. Although Boysen created it, Walter Knott of Knott's Berry Farm gets the credit for introducing it to the public.

Knott's Berry Farm, Buena Park, California

Walt Disney's Great Big idea

When people talk about amusement parks, the name *Disney* always seems to come up. Why? It is because of a man named Walt Disney. He changed the history of amusement parks.

Who Is Mortimer Mouse?

Mickey Mouse might have been Mortimer Mouse if it weren't for Walt Disney's wife, Lillian. She thought the name was too fancy and suggested *Mickey* instead. Walt Disney himself was the voice of Mickey for almost 20 years.

Mickey Mouse Is Born

Walt Disney always loved drawing. He took art classes as a young boy. By the time he was 18 years old, he had a job as an illustrator. Disney then moved to California. He opened a business with his brother, Roy. It was called Disney Brothers Studio. They were joined by another illustrator, Ub Iwerks. The studio made short cartoons that were shown in movie theaters. In 1928, Walt Disney and Iwerks created Mickey Mouse. He was the star of a film called *Steamboat Willie*. Mickey is now one of the most famous cartoon characters of all time.

Moving into Movies

The Disney Studio was very successful. Walt Disney and his partners invented new and better ways to create **animated** films. In 1937, the studio produced the first movie-length animated cartoon ever made in the United States. It was *Snow White and the Seven Dwarfs*. The movie was very popular. The studio went on to produce many more popular animated movies. It produced **live-action** movies as well.

Walt Disney shares an animation plan.

Disneyland: TV Show and Place

Walt Disney had an idea for an amusement park. It would be a theme park. Visitors would experience the magic of Disney movies. He needed money to pay for the theme park. So, he made deals to create television shows.

This was in the 1950s. TV was very new. There was no color TV, and there were only three TV channels. Disney's TV show was called *Disneyland*. It first aired in 1954. The weekly show had themes based on sections Disney was creating in his amusement park. The themes were: Adventureland, Fantasyland, Frontierland, and Tomorrowland.

In 1955, Disneyland opened in California. The opening ceremony was shown live on TV. It was watched by almost half of all Americans. Walt Disney called Disneyland "the happiest place on Earth." At first, visitors paid one dollar to get into the park. Tickets for rides were extra. They cost between 10 and 35 cents each.

The Mickey Mouse Club

The Mickey Mouse Club was a daily TV series created by Walt Disney. It first aired in 1955. The "Mouseketeers" were young actors and actresses who sang and danced, usually wearing mouse ears. The show had a different theme for each day of the week.

guests and attractions at Disneyland

Disneyland was a huge success. It became a popular place for family vacations. Americans love it. People from around the world come as well. About a century after Walt Disney introduced Mickey Mouse to the world, Disney's big idea is still going strong.

Walt Disney World

Walt Disney's vision did not stop at Disneyland. He had an idea for another Disney park. This one would be in Florida. He started buying the land to make it happen. But before he could make this new dream come true, Disney died in 1966. His brother, Roy Disney, stepped in to run the company. He did not let his brother's dream die. He was in charge when the new Disney theme park, Walt Disney World, opened in Florida in 1971.

Walt Disney World had one theme park at the time. It was called the Magic Kingdom. Today, there are three theme parks, two water parks, and EPCOT. EPCOT is a special part of Walt Disney's vision. It invites visitors to learn about countries around the world.

By the year 2021, there were 12 Disney theme parks across six Disney resorts, with more than 50 hotels around the world. There are even Disney **cruise ships**. They take travelers to many places in the world, including a private Disney island. Disney movies, both animated and live-action, remain very popular. Mickey Mouse remains the face of Disney amusement parks around the world.

EPCOT

Disney cruise ship

Disney Scents

Disney theme parks control every detail of the visitor's experience. Throughout Disneyland and Disney World, there are hidden **devices** called "Smellitzers" that pump out a scent, similar to how an air freshener works. Depending on the place, visitors might smell vanilla, popcorn, pastries, or even burning wood.

Top Amusement Parks

The United States has many different amusement parks. All of them are lots of fun. It is impossible to say which one is the "best." Here are some that are very popular with many people.

The Disney Parks: Tops in Attendance

Disney parks take the top five spots as the most popular theme parks in the United States. The Magic Kingdom at Walt Disney World in Florida is number 1 for most visitors in a year. Disneyland in California is number 2. They are followed by Disney's Animal Kingdom, EPCOT, and Hollywood Studios. These last three are in Florida.

Six Flags: Not Just Texas Anymore

Six Flags Over Texas opened in 1961. Its theme comes from the fact that six different nations have claimed the land that is now Texas in the past. The Texas park was just the beginning. The **developer** had the idea to build theme parks in different regions of the country. Visitors would not have to travel far to have a great time at a theme park. Today, Six Flags operates parks in the United States, Canada, and Mexico. They are all very popular.

Those Six Flags

During its history, these six nations have claimed to rule all or part of what is now Texas: Spain, France, Mexico, Republic of Texas, United States of America, and Confederate States of America.

Six Flags Over Texas, Arlington, Texas

Universal Studios: Experience the Show

Universal is a company that makes movies and TV shows. It also has theme parks in California, Florida, Japan, and Singapore. What is the theme? Movies and TV shows, of course! Are you a Harry Potter fan? Or maybe you really like Spongebob, Minions, Dr. Seuss, or Shrek. You will find them there. There are other TV and movie characters and places, too. The roller coasters, other rides, and visitors' experiences relate to movies and TV. They actually make movies and TV shows at Universal Studios in California. Visitors there can tour sets and learn about how movies are made.

The Wizarding World of Harry Potter at Universal Orlando

Jurassic Park attraction at Universal Studios, Singapore

Dollywood: Mountain Magic

Dollywood gets its name from Dolly Parton. The singer and actress is one of this Tennessee park's owners. The theme is inspired by her background. She grew up nearby in the Smoky Mountains. This park has a lot of country charm. It also has plenty of fun. There are thrilling roller coasters, a beautiful carousel, and many other fun rides. There's a water park, too, as well as theaters, a museum, and great southern food. Dollywood has many musical performances. It also has special festivals each year. One celebrates **bluegrass music** and barbecue. Another celebrates the cultures of other nations.

Grist Mill, Dollywood

Dollywood Is Also for the Birds

Some amazing birds are part of the experience at Dollywood. Visitors can attend a show that allows them to get close to and learn about **birds of prey**. The Eagle Mountain Sanctuary is home to bald eagles that are cared for by the American Eagle Foundation.

Silver Dollar City: Mining for Fun

Silver Dollar City is in Missouri. This park with an old mining town theme opened in 1960. It looks like a town that might have existed there in the 1880s. It has a **blacksmith** shop, a general store, and an ice cream store. There are craft demonstrations, festivals, shows, and restaurants, too. This park also has extra-modern attractions, of course. Its roller coasters have names such as Wildfire, Outlaw Run, and Time Traveler.

A Silver Dollar City blacksmith works with heated metal.

A Silver Dollar Tradition

Early visitors to Silver Dollar City would receive a real silver dollar as change when they paid the admission fee. When they spent the silver dollar outside the park, people might ask where it came from. That is how the park attracted new visitors without paying for advertising.

A Busch Gardens giraffe greets visitors.

roller coaster at Busch Gardens, Florida

Busch Gardens: Visiting Africa and Europe

Busch Gardens has two parks in the United States. One is in Florida, and one is in Virginia. Visitors in Florida can see free-roaming herds of African animals. They can even hand-feed flamingos. Roller coasters and other rides reflect the African theme. Europe is the theme at Busch Gardens in Virginia. It has been voted the world's most beautiful theme park for more than 30 years in a row. It has several very exciting roller coasters. Both parks have rides that are less scary but lots of fun. In either park, you might run into some familiar faces from a place called Sesame Street.

Thrills, Spills, and Chills

Amusement parks have gone through tremendous **transformation** from the simple village fairs of 1,000 years ago. Today, they amaze us with their size, technology, and beauty. They thrill and inspire people of all ages. They definitely "amuse," which is exactly what their name tells us they are designed to do. We smile, we laugh, and sometimes we even scream. We also learn about other people and places, how things work, what the past was like, and what the future might hold.

Engineers design thrilling rides and attractions.

Coney Island, New York

The next time you go to an amusement park, whether it is big or small, take a really close look. Notice the big things like the rides and the buildings. What makes the machinery work? Who could have designed and built those amazing **structures**? Also, pay attention to the small things. What gets your attention, and why? How do the colors shape your experience? How do you know what is where and how to get there? Do you hear music? What jobs are workers doing, and why does it matter?

When you look closely, you will see that every amusement park tells a story. It is almost always a story of creativity and hard work. People with big ideas and dreams are behind everything you do and see there.

Fun Requires Work

Every amusement park needs people to make the fun happen. There are people who take tickets, manage the rides, cook food, and clean the parks. But there are thousands of jobs you never see. These include office workers, inventors, construction workers, artists, and many more!

Map It!

Which amusement parks would you like to visit? In this activity, you and your group will choose five amusement parks that you would like to go to. Then, you will plan the route to get you there.

Here are the steps:

1. With your group, choose five amusement parks featured in this book that you would like to visit. Each park must be in a different state. One can be in the state where you live. If you disagree on which parks to go to, talk it through or take a vote to come to an agreement.
2. Plan a road trip to take you to each of those parks. Work together to figure out the shortest route possible. Your trip should include driving from where you are now to each of the amusement parks and then back home again.
3. Make a map showing your route. In addition to the amusement parks, show any large cities you will pass through on the way. Also show the location of the capital of each state you pass through.

Morey's Piers,
Wildwood, New Jersey

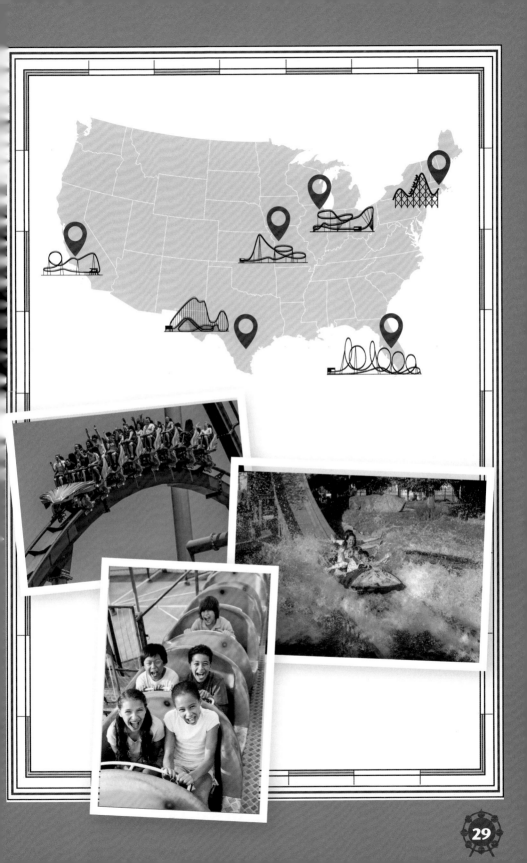

Glossary

agriculture—the science of farming

animated—created from a series of drawings or pictures that are shown one after another so they appear to move

birds of prey—birds that hunt and eat other animals

blacksmith—a person who makes or repairs things made of iron

bluegrass music—music made with instruments, such as the banjo, fiddle, or guitar, with people singing in harmony

cruise ships—large ships that take many people at a time on a trip

developer—a person or company that builds and sells houses and other properties

devices—things that have been made to be used for a special purpose

exposition—a public show or exhibition

fee—an amount of money paid for a specific experience or service

flume—a sloping channel for moving water

live-action—using actors rather than animation

silver dollar—a large silver coin worth one dollar

slopes—parts of the ground or structures that slant downward

stroll—to walk slowly in a relaxed way

structures—objects built by putting parts together and that stand on their own

transformation—a complete change in someone's or something's appearance

Index

Santa Cruz Beach Boardwalk, California

Learn More!

Each amusement park begins with a dream and a vision. Someone has to make it happen! Learn more about one of these dreamers and visionaries.

- Select an amusement park and the person who started it.
- Research to find out more about that person. What gave them the idea? How did they get started? What troubles did they have? Who helped them along the way?
- Once you have the information, make a poster to show the person's journey from idea to amusement park. Print or draw pictures to bring your poster to life.

the upside-down WonderWorks venue on the harbor of Broadway at the Beach, South Carolina